100 Most Famous People in History

Melissa Ackerman

PUBLISHED BY:

Melissa Ackerman

Copyright © 2016

Disclaimer

The information contained in this book is for general information purposes only. The information is provided by the authors and, while we endeavor to keep the information up to date and correct, we make no representations or warranties of any kind, expressed or implied, about the completeness, accuracy, reliability, suitability or availability with respect to the book or the information, products, services, or related graphics contained in the book for any purpose. Any reliance you place on such information is therefore strictly at your own risk.

TABLE OF CONTENTS

Abraham

Abraham or Abram (1800 BCE – 1600 BCE), is considered as the first of the three patriarchs of Judaism – the ancestors of the Israelites comprised by Abraham, his son Isaac and Isaac's son Jacob. In the Bible, he is known for having an unswerving faith in God. In fact, when God tests Abraham's faith in Him by demanding that he sacrifices his firstborn son, Isaac, Abraham does not hesitate. He takes Isaac up to the top of a mountain and is about to slay him when an angel arrives and tells him to stop. God is greatly impressed with Abraham's faith and so, He blesses him and gave him the Promised Land – the land from the river of Egypt to the great river, the Euphrates which was promised and given by God to Abraham and his descendants.

Ramesses II

Ramesses II or Ramses, or Ramesses the Great was born on 1303 BC and died July or August 1213 BC at the age of around 90 or 91. He was the third Egyptian Pharaoh, reigning from 1279 BC to 1213 BC. He is regarded as the most celebrated, most powerful and the greatest of all pharaoh of the Egyptian Empire. During his reign, he was focused on building cities, temples and monuments. In addition, Ramesses II is also known as Ozymandias in Greek, which means, "The justice of Rê is powerful – chosen of Rê". The mummy of Ramesses II is now on display in the Cairo Museum.

Homer

Homer is believed to have lived around 850 BCE or later. BCE (Before Common Era) and BC (Before Christ) are just the same, referring to the years before Christ was born. He is very well known as the author of the *Iliad* and the *Odyssey* – two ancient Greek epic poems or lengthy poems about heroic deeds and events significant to a culture or nation. The ancient Greeks also regarded him as the first and greatest of all the poets. In addition, he is also described by Greeks as the: "first teacher", of tragedy, the "leader of learning", and the one who "has taught Greece". Most of Homer's works show persuasive speaking and writing.

Gautama Buddha

Gautama Buddha, who is also known as Siddhartha Gautama, or simply the Buddha was a prince born in northern India. Despite being a royalty, Gautama Buddha gave up his wealth and the comforts of the palace to seek enlightenment. After attaining what was called, Nirvana (highest state that someone can attain, a state of enlightenment), he spent all of his remaining life in teaching other people about Nirvana. Gautama Buddha is very well known as the founder of Buddhism. He is regarded by Buddhists as the enlightened one, or the divine teacher who attained full Buddhahood (a rank of a Buddha).

Confucius

Confucius (born on September 28, 551 and died in 479 BC) was a Chinese politician, teacher and philosopher. His writings about justice, life and society were later developed into Confucianism – a system of philosophical and ethical teachings. Interestingly, the principles of Confucius were based on Chinese traditions and beliefs such as, strong family loyalty, ancestor worship and respect for elders as well as for husbands. He even regarded family as a basis for ideal government. Confucius is popularly known as the proponent of the Golden Rule: "Do not do to others what you do not want done to yourself".

Socrates

Socrates (469 BC–399 BC) was a Greek philosopher who contributed a lot to the development of Western philosophy and political thought. One of his famous students was Plato. However, Socrates is most famous for his Socratic method of self-enquiry – a form of dialogue between individuals, based on asking and answering questions to draw out ideas and underlying presumptions from the questioned person.

Plato

Plato (424 – 348 BC) was another Greek philosopher. His teacher was the renowned Socrates. On the other hand, Plato himself was also a teacher and Aristotle was his most famous student. Moreover, Plato was the one who founded the Academy in Athens. His writings, especially, 'The Republic' became the basis of early Western philosophy. In addition to being an important contributor in Western science, philosophy, and mathematics, Plato has also often been regarded as one of the founders of Western religion and spirituality, as it was him who considered the idea of people's existence, the nature of reality and the notion of the soul.

Aristotle

Aristotle (384 BC – 322 BC) was Greek philosopher and a scientist. He was the teacher of Alexander the Great. Aristotle was already eighteen years old when he joined Plato's Academy in Athens. When Plato died, Aristotle left Athens and tutored Alexander the Great at the request of Philip of Macedon. Aristotle's writings tackle many subjects like: biology, physics, logic, zoology, poetry, aesthetics, metaphysics, ethics, theater, music, linguistics, politics and government.

Alexander the Great

Alexander the Great or Alexander III of Macedon (356 – 323 BC) was the king of Macedonia, an Ancient Greek kingdom. He was only 20 years old when he took the throne and became the king after his father's assassination. Most of his years as the king were spent on a military campaign all over Asia and northeast Africa. And so, after 10 years, Alexander the Great was able to create one of the largest empires of the ancient world – from Greece to India. As one of history's most successful military commanders, Alexander the Great was undefeated in battle. Today, military academies all over the world still teach his tactics and strategies. He is also often regarded as one of the most influential people in history.

Archimedes

Archimedes of Syracuse (287 B.C – 212) was an Ancient Greek mathematician, physicist, astronomer and inventor. He is well known for his contributions to mathematics. He also explained many scientific principles and even invented contraptions like, Archimedes screw or screw pump – a machine used for transferring water from a low-lying body of water into irrigation ditches or for draining water out of mines. Universally, Archimedes is noted as the greatest mathematician of the ancient times. Some of his mathematical achievements include: the area of a circle, the surface area and volume of a sphere, and the area under a parabola. Unfortunately, Archimedes died during the siege of Syracuse when he was killed by a Roman soldier, despite orders that he should not be harmed.

Julius Caesar

Gaius Julius Caesar or Julius Caesar (13 July 100 BC – 15 March 44 BC) was a Roman politician and military commander who conquered Gaul and England to expand the Roman Empire. Due to his military strength, he became an Emperor of Rome from 49 BC, until his assassination in 44BC. During his reign as the emperor, Caesar began social and governmental reforms, including the creation of the Julian calendar. The Julian calendar is a calendar introduced by Julius Caesar in 46 BC, in which the year consisted of 365 days and 366 days every fourth year. Just like Alexander the Great, Caesar is considered by many historians as one of the greatest military commanders in history.

Cleopatra

Cleopatra or Cleopatra VII Philopator (69 – 30 BC) was the last member of the Ptolemaic dynasty that became the Pharaoh of Egypt. The Ptolemaic dynasty was a family of Macedonian Greek origin that ruled Egypt after Alexander the Great's death. However, Cleopatra learned to speak Egyptian and represented herself as the reincarnation of the Egyptian goddess Isis. As the ruler of Egypt, Cleopatra bravely defended the country from the expanding Roman Empire. In doing so she formed relationships with two of Rome's most powerful leaders Marc Anthony and Julius Caesar. When Cleopatra died, her son, Caesarion shortly ruled Egypt. However, Caesarion was killed and Egypt became a province of the Roman Empire.

Moses

Moses was a prophet who was a former Egyptian prince that became a religious leader. He was also a lawgiver, to whom the Ten Commandments of God was given, making him one of the most important prophets. According to the Book of Exodus, he was born at a time when his people, the Israelites, were enslaved by the Egyptians. His mother secretly hid him when the Pharaoh ordered all newborn Hebrew boys to be killed. Later on, the child (Moses) was adopted as a foundling from the Nile River and grew up with the Egyptian royal family. After killing an Egyptian, Moses fled across the Red Sea. However, God sent Moses back to Egypt to lead the freedom of Israelites from slavery. Moses brought Israelites out of Egypt and across the Red Sea. However, after 40 years of wandering in the desert, Moses suddenly died.

Mary Magdalene

Mary Magdalene or Mary of Magdala or simply, Magdalene, is a figure in Christianity who, according to the Bible, was one of Jesus' followers. It is said the she witnessed Jesus' crucifixion. She is also said to be present two days later, when Jesus was resurrected. In addition, Mary Magdalene is considered by the Catholic, Eastern Orthodox, Anglican, and Lutheran churches as a saint, with July 22 as her feast day.

Jesus Christ

Jesus Christ or Jesus of Nazareth (c.5BC – 30AD) is an important figure of Christianity and a spiritual teacher, preaching his message orally. He is regarded by Christian as the Messiah (leader and savior) predicted in the Old Testament. Christians also believed that Jesus Christ is the Son of God – conceived by the Holy Spirit and was born of a virgin named Mary. Due to his preaching, Jesus was arrested, tried by the Jewish authorities and then crucified to his death by the order of Pontius Pilate (a Roman leader). After his death, his followers believed that Jesus was resurrected and the community they formed eventually became the Christian Church. The widely used calendar era "AD", or "Anno Domini" and "CE" or "Common Era", refers to the year after Christ was born).

St Paul

Saint Paul or Paul the Apostle (5 – AD 67) was a Jewish and a Roman citizen who converted to Christianity. As his name suggests, he was an apostle (not one of the Twelve Apostles) who taught the gospel or life, death, and resurrection of Jesus of Nazareth during the 1st-century. As a Jew and a Roman citizen, he was able to teach both Jewish and Roman audiences. In fact, his writings and teachings play a significant role in helping the spread of Christianity.

Judas Iscariot

Judas Iscariot was one of the twelve original disciples of Jesus Christ. He is well known for the kiss and betrayal of Jesus in exchange of thirty silver coins. Today, his name is often associated with betrayal. Though there are varied written accounts of his death, the most popular version is that Judas hanged himself after his betrayal of Jesus. Despite the negativity of what he has done, he remains a controversial figure in Christian history. His betrayal is seen as the trigger that led to Jesus' Crucifixion and Resurrection, in which, according to traditional Christian theology, brought salvation to humanity.

Marcus Aurelius

Marcus Aurelius (26 April 121 – 17 March 180) was a Roman Emperor from 161 to 180, and is regarded as the last of the so-called Five Good Emperors (Roman emperors which include: Nerva, Trajan, Hadrian, Antoninus Pius and Marcus Aurelius). He was a practitioner of Stoicism or an ancient Greek school of philosophy which taught that virtue is based on knowledge. His writing, which is known as the Meditations of Marcus Aurelius, is the most important source of today's modern understanding of this ancient philosophy.

Constantine the Great

Constantine the Great (27 February 272 – 22 May 337) became a Roman Emperor after his father's death in the year 306. He was considered as the first Roman Emperor to embrace Christianity. In fact, it was during his reign when the Edict of Milan, which decreed tolerance for Christianity in the empire, was proclaimed. Prior to the Edict, Christians were persecuted because of their faith. In addition, Constantine also became famous after he ended victorious in a series of civil wars against the other Roman emperors, Maxentius and Licinius (rival of Constantine) to become sole ruler of both west and east.

Charlemagne

Charlemagne, or Charles the Great (2 April 742 – 28 January 814) was the King of Franks and Emperor of the Romans. Since the fall of the Roman Empire, he was able to unify a large part of Europe for the first time. And so, he was called the "Father of Europe". It was in 800 when Charlemagne was crowned Emperor of the Romans that he reached the height of his power. The coronation was done by Pope Leo III on Christmas Day at the Old St. Peter's Basilica. The emperor died in 814, just about 14 years after he was crowned. Today, his remains were laid to rest in Germany.

Saladin

An-Nasir Salah ad-Din Yusuf ibn Ayyub, who is also known as Saladin (1138 – 1193) is the first sultan of Egypt and Syria and the leader of the Arabs during the Crusades, a series of religious wars or holy wars. These wars were wars caused by differences in religion. He unified Muslim provinces and provided effective military opposition to the Christian crusades. After winning the battle in 1187, Saladin died in Damascus in 1193. During this time, he had given away much of his personal wealth to his subjects. Aside from being popular in Muslim, Arab, Turkish and Kurdish culture, Saladin has also been described as being the most famous Kurd (an ethnic group in the Middle East) in history.

Thomas Aquinas

Thomas Aquinas (1225 – 1274) was a Roman Catholic priest, philosopher and theologian. In addition, he is also known as Doctor of the Church – a title given by the Catholic Church to saints who have significant contributions to theology or doctrine. More importantly, Thomas Aquinas is honored by the Catholic Church as a saint and a model teacher for those who are studying for the priesthood and is considered as one of the greatest philosopher and theologian. He is best known for writing *Summa Theologiae*, a compendium about teachings of the Catholic Church.

Marco Polo

Marco Polo (1254 – 1324) was a Venetian explorer who traveled to Asia and China. His travels were recorded in the *Book of the Marvels of the World*, or *The Travels of Marco Polo*, which introduced Europeans to Central Asia and China. Along with his father and uncle, Marco Polo travelled through Asia in 1269. After 24 years, they return to Venice, only to find the city was at war with Genoa. Because of the war, Marco Polo was imprisoned, but was released in 1299. He then became a wealthy merchant, got married and had three children. In 1324, he died and was buried in the church of San Lorenzo in his home city – Venice.

Johannes Gutenberg

Johannes Gensfleisch zur Laden zum Gutenberg, or simply Johannes Gutenberg (1395 – 1468) was a German inventor, printer and publisher who introduced printing to Europe. This introduction of mechanical printing eventually led to the start of the Printing Revolution or the Printing Press – a machine that allowed the mass production of printed books and or any printed materials. Universally, this invention by Johannes Gutenberg was regarded as the most important invention of the second millennium. His major work, the Gutenberg Bible or the 42-line Bible (a Bible with 42 lines of print on each page) was the first major book printed using the said invention.

Joan of Arc

Joan of Arc (6 January 1412 – 30 May 1431) was a young peasant girl who became a French Saint. She was a heroine who led French forces during the Lancastrian phase of the Hundred Years' War. The Hundred Years' War is a series of conflicts from 1337 to 1453 by the Kingdom of England, against the Kingdom of France, for control of the Kingdom of France. The Lancastrian phase, on the other hand, was the third phase of the said war that lasted from 1415 to 1453. On 23 May 1430, Joan of Arc was captured by the enemy and was put on trial for a variety of charges. After she was declared guilty, she was burned on 30 May 1431, dying at about nineteen years of age. In 1456, her case was examined and she was pronounced innocent of the charges against her. And so, in the 16th century Joan of Arc became a symbol of the Catholic League. She was also declared a national symbol of France in 1803, by the decision of Napoleon Bonaparte.

Christopher Columbus

Christopher Columbus (1451 – 1506) was an Italian explorer and navigator who landed in America. Under the financial support and guidance of the Catholic Monarchs of Spain, he completed four voyages across the Atlantic Ocean. Columbus then proposed to reach the East Indies by sailing westward. Eventually his proposal was supported by the Spanish Crown which was looking for a chance to enter the spice trade with Asia through a new westward route. However, in 1492, Columbus reached the New World or the Americas instead of Japan as he had intended. He landed on an island in the Bahamas which he named "San Salvador". Unfortunately, Columbus was not the first one who reached America. However, Columbus is the one who open the opportunity for Europeans to enter the Americas.

Leonardo da Vinci

Leonardo di ser Piero da Vinci, who is more commonly known as Leonardo da Vinci (15 April 1452 – 2 May 1519) was an Italian scientist, artist, and polymath. He is famous for painting the *Mona Lisa* and *the Last Supper*. The Mona Lisa is the most famous and most parodied portrait, while The Last Supper is the most reproduced religious painting of all time. Because of these iconic paintings, Leonardo da Vinci is widely considered as one of the greatest painters of all time.

Martin Luther

Martin Luther (10 November 1483 – 18 February 1546) was a German professor of theology, a composer, a priest and an important figure in the Protestant Reformation –a schism or division from the Roman Catholic Church. The reform started when Martin Luther opposed the power of the Pope and rejected several teachings and practices of the Roman Catholic Church. According to him, salvation and eternal life are not earned by good deeds but are received only as free gift of God's grace through the believer's faith in Jesus Christ as redeemer from sin. Because of his confrontation and rejection of the teachings of the Roman Catholic Church, Martin Luther was condemned as an outlaw by the Holy Roman Emperor Charles V.

William Tyndale

William Tyndale (1494 – 1536) was an English scholar who became a leading figure in the Protestant Reformation. He became popular for translating the Bible into English. This translation was the first English Bible to be drawn directly from Hebrew and Greek texts. Unfortunately, as a leader of the Protestant reform, Tyndale was arrested, jailed and convicted of heresy or contradicting the Christian doctrine. He was executed by strangulation and then burnt. Today, the Tyndale Bible continued to play a significant role in spreading Reformation ideas across the English-speaking world.

Sir Walter Raleigh

Sir Walter Raleigh (1552 – 1618) was an English explorer, writer, poet, soldier and politician. He made several journeys to the Americas. He is also well known for popularizing tobacco in England. The most compelling story about his life started in 1594, when he learned about the "City of Gold", which is also called "El Dorado" in South America. He then sailed to find it, while recording the account of his experiences in a book that contributed to the legend of "El Dorado". However, his voyage was unsuccessful, and men under his command ransacked a Spanish outpost. He returned to England and, to patch things up with the Spanish, Raleigh was arrested and executed in 1618.

Galileo Galilei

Galileo Galilei (15 February 1564 – 8 January 1642) was an Italian astronomer, physicist, engineer, philosopher, and mathematician who developed the modern telescope and proved that the earth revolved around the sun. He has been called the "father of observational astronomy", as well as the "father of modern physics" and the "father of science". With the help of the telescope that he developed, Galileo Galilei discovered the four largest satellites of Jupiter or the Galilean moons. Another significant contribution of Galileo, aside from the telescope, is his invention of improved military compass.

William Shakespeare

William Shakespeare (1564- 1616) was an English poet, playwright, and actor. He is noted as the greatest writer in the English language. He had so many written works, but the most popular ones are: *Romeo and Juliet, Hamlet, Macbeth* and *Othello*. Overall, his works include: 38 plays, 154 sonnets, two long narrative poems, and a few other verses. His plays have been translated into every major language and are performed all over the world more often compared to those of any other playwright. His road to stardom began in London between 1585 and 1592, when he became a successful actor, writer, and part-owner of a playing company called the Lord Chamberlain's Men, or the King's Men. He retired in 1613, at age 49. Three years later, William Shakespeare died.

Rene Descartes

René Descartes (31 March 1596 – 11 February 1650) was a French philosopher, mathematician, and scientist. He is regarded as the father of modern philosophy. His most significant contribution in mathematics is the Cartesian coordinate system — in simple terms, a way to pinpoint where you are on a graph by how far along, and how far up or down the point is. Aside from the Cartesian coordinate system, Rene Descartes is also known for his philosophical statement: "Cogito ergo sum" which means, "I think, therefore I am".

Sir Isaac Newton

Sir Isaac Newton (25 December 1642 – 20 March 1727) was an English mathematician and scientist. He is regarded as one of the most influential scientists of all time and was well recognized for his laws of motion and gravity, which states the relationship between motion and gravity. Aside from the Newton's Law of Motion, Sir Isaac Newton also built the first practical reflecting telescope. He also developed a theory of color based on the observation that when a white light hits a prism, the light that passes through it decomposes into many colors.

Voltaire

François-Marie Arouet, who is more commonly known as Voltaire (21 November 1694 – 30 May 1778) was a French philosopher, writer and historian. He became popular due to his attacks on the Catholic Church, as well as due to his advocacy of freedom of religion, freedom of expression and separation of church and state. As a versatile writer, he has written in almost every literary form like plays, poems, novels, essays, and historical and scientific works. Overall, he has more than 20,000 letters and more than 2,000 books and pamphlets.

Catherine the Great

Catherine II of Russia who is also known as Catherine the Great (1729 – 1796) was a Russian Queen that reigned from 1762 until her death in 1796. She was considered as the most renowned and the longest-ruling female leader of Russia. During her reign, Russia became a major European power. She became the queen after her husband, Peter III, was assassinated. It was also during her reign when many new cities and towns were founded. In addition, the period of Catherine the Great's rule, called the Catherinian Era, is often considered the Golden Age of the Russian Empire.

George Washington

George Washington (1732 – 1799) was the first President of the United States of America, from 1789 to 1797. He also served as the Commander-in-Chief of the Continental Army during the American Revolutionary War and one of the Founding Fathers of the United States. Due to his contributions, he is called the "father of his country". George Washington was admired for his strong leadership qualities. While in power, he pursued the preservation of liberty, reduction of regional tensions, as well as the promotion of American nationalism. Upon his death, Washington was eulogized as "first in war, first in peace, and first in the hearts of his countrymen". He is also considered as one of the top three presidents in American history.

Thomas Paine

Thomas Paine (1737–1809) was an English-American author and philosopher. Just like George Washington, he is also one of the Founding Fathers of the United States. He is noted as the writer of *'Common Sense'* (1776) and the *Rights of Man* (1791) – the two most influential pamphlets at the start of the American Revolution that inspired the rebels in 1776 to declare independence from Britain. Due to his writings, he was arrested and was taken to Luxembourg Prison in Paris in 1793. While in prison, he continued to work on The Age of Reason (1793–94), a pamphlet where he argued against Christian doctrine. In 1794, Paine was release with the help of James Monroe, the fifth president of the USA. In 1802, Paine returned to the U.S. where he died.

Thomas Jefferson

Thomas Jefferson (1743- 1826) was the third President of the United States of America. He passed laws on religious tolerance in his state of Virginia and founded the University of Virginia. He is well known as a proponent of democracy, republicanism, and individual rights. He also pursued the nation's shipping and trade interests. However, during Thomas Jefferson's second term as the US president, he was beset with difficulties. His only full-length book, "Notes on the State of Virginia" (1785), is considered the most important American book published before 1800.

Wolfgang Amadeus Mozart

Wolfgang Amadeus Mozart (27 January 1756 – 5 December 1791) was an Austrian music composer. He is widely regarded as one of the greatest musical geniuses of all time. In fact, at the age of five, He was able to compose music and perform before European royalty. During his entire life, he composed more than 600 works, making him one of the most popular classical composers. Interestingly, Ludwig van Beethoven, another great music composer was inspired by Mozart's works.

William Wilberforce

William Wilberforce (1759 – 1833) was an English politician, philanthropist campaigner against slavery. He was the leader of the movement that helped abolish slavery in 1833. He began his life as a politician in 1780 as a Member of Parliament or representative for Yorkshire. In 1785, William Wilberforce became an Evangelical Christian, which resulted in major changes to his lifestyle and a lifelong concern for reform. He also became convinced of the importance of religion, morality and education.

Napoleon Bonaparte

Napoléon Bonaparte (15 August 1769 – 5 May 1821) was a French military and political leader. He was the one who made France a major European power. He was also the Emperor of the French from 1804 to 1815. In the Napoleonic Wars (series of major global conflicts between French Empire and other European powers), Napoleon Bonaparte dominated and won most of the wars, as well as the other battles. And so, he is considered as one of the greatest commanders in history. In fact, his wars and war tactics are studied at military schools all over the world.

Ludwig van Beethoven

Ludwig van Beethoven (17 December 1770 – 26 March 1827) was a German music composer. He is considered as one of the most famous and influential of all composers. At an early age, he already displayed his musical talents. He was taught by his father Johann van Beethoven and by Christian Gottlob Neefe, a composer and conductor. At the age of 21 Beethoven moved to Vienna where he studied composition and gained a reputation as an excellent pianist. By his late 20s, Beethoven's hearing began to deteriorate, which eventually led to his being almost totally deaf. In 1811 he stopped conducting and performing in public but continued to compose. His best-known compositions include: *the Fifth Symphony* and *the Ninth Symphony*.

Abraham Lincoln

Abraham Lincoln (12 February 1809 – 15 April 1865) was the 16th President of the United States of America. He led the northern Union army that fought to protect the Union (USA) during the American Civil War. By leading the Union forces, Lincoln was able to preserve the Union, abolished slavery, strengthened the US government and modernized the economy. However, on April 14, 1865, Lincoln was assassinated by John Wilkes Booth, an American stage actor. Abraham Lincoln was ranked as one of the three greatest U.S. presidents.

Charles Darwin

Charles Robert Darwin, or simply, Charles Darwin (12 February 1809 – 19 April 1882) was an English naturalist and geologist who developed the theory of evolution. Through his book 'The Origin of Species' (1859) he cited that all species of life have descended over time from common ancestors. By the 1870s, many people had accepted evolution as a fact. This discovery by Charles Darwin is the unifying theory of life sciences, explaining the diversity of life. And because of his contribution, Darwin has been regarded as one of the most influential figures in human history.

Karl Marx

Karl Marx (5 May 1818 – 14 March 1883) was a philosopher, economist, sociologist, and journalist. He is very well known as the author of *Das Kapital*, in which he explained that the poor people should get together and demands that they owned the factories they worked in, be paid better by the rich people and have rights and a normal life too. The said book became a bestseller and many people were inspired by his thoughts. And so, with his works, Karl Marx was noted as one of the principal architects of modern sociology and social science.

Queen Victoria

Queen Victoria or Alexandrina Victoria (24 May 1819 – 22 January 1901) is the Queen of the United Kingdom of Great Britain and Ireland from 20 June 1837 until her death in 1901. She also became the Empress of India from 1 May 1876 until 22 January 1901. She was only 18 when she became the queen, after her father's three elder brothers had all died. Publicly, she became a national icon who was identified with strict standards of personal morality. In 1840, Victoria married her first cousin, Prince Albert and had nine children. However, in 1861, after her husband's death, Victoria plunged into deep mourning and avoided public appearances. Generally, her reign of 63 years and seven months which is known as the Victorian Era was a period of industrial, cultural, political, scientific, and military change within the United Kingdom. Her era was also marked by a great expansion of the British Empire.

Florence Nightingale

Florence Nightingale (12 May 1820 – 13 August 1910) was an English social reformer and statistician. She was the founder of modern nursing. She became famous during the Crimean War, as she was the one who organized the caring for wounded soldiers. She became an icon and is known as "The Lady with the Lamp", making rounds on wounded soldiers at night. In 1860, she laid the foundation of professional nursing with the establishment of her nursing school at St Thomas' Hospital in London. To commemorate her works in nursing, the Nightingale Pledge taken by new nurses, and the Florence Nightingale Medal, the highest international distinction a nurse can achieve, were named in her honor.

Louis Pasteur

Louis Pasteur (27 December 1822 – 28 September 1895) was a French chemist and biologist known for his contributions on vaccination, microbial fermentation and pasteurization. He was the one who developed vaccines for rabies and anthrax. He also developed pasteurization – the process of making milk safer. This process (pasteurization) which involves techniques of treating milk and wine to stop bacterial contamination, made Louis Pasteur popular to the general public. Generally, his breakthroughs and discoveries in the causes and preventions of diseases have saved countless lives ever since, especially those who are victims of anthrax and rabies.

Leo Tolstoy

Count Lev Nikolayevich Tolstoy or simply, Leo Tolstoy (1828 – 1910) was a Russian writer and philosopher, who is considered as one of the greatest authors of all time. He is also a social activist – promoting non-violence and equality in society. What made Tolstoy popular were his epic novels entitled, 'War and Peace' (1869) and 'Anna Karenina' (1877). War and Peace is one of the longest novels ever written and is all about spirituality and family happiness. On the other hand, Anna Karenina, is a very popular novel about the importance of love and its place in a marriage. Overall, Leo Tolstoy's works includes short stories, novellas, plays and philosophical essays.

Thomas Alva Edison

Thomas Alva Edison (11 February 1847 – 18 October 1931) was an American inventor and businessman who developed the electric light bulb. He also formed a company to make electricity available to ordinary homes. Aside from the light bulb, he also developed the phonograph, the motion picture camera, a mechanical vote recorder and a battery for an electric car. In addition, Edison is considered as one of the first inventors to mass produce his inventions. For the record, he holds around 1,093 US patents to his name.

Vincent van Gogh

Vincent Willem van Gogh, or simply Vincent van Gogh (30 March 1853 – 29 July 1890) was a Dutch painter. He is regarded as one of the most famous and influential figures in the history of Western art. He created about 2100 artworks, most of which were created in the last two years of his life. One of his most popular paintings is *The Starry Night*. Typically, his subjects for painting includes: landscapes, portraits and self-portraits. Vincent van Gogh was only able to sold one painting during his lifetime. His fame just started after his death, at the aged of 37, due to poverty and mental illness.

Oscar Wilde

Oscar Fingal O'Flahertie Wills Wilde or simply, Oscar Wilde (16 October 1854 – 30 November 1900) was an Irish writer noted for his wit, flamboyant dress and charm, that made him one of the best-known personalities of his day. He wrote in different forms including: poems, novels, essays and plays. He is best remembered for his novel, 'The Picture of Dorian Gray', a novel that is about beauty or aesthetics. Unfortunately, Oscar Wilde was convicted and imprisoned for two years. Upon his release, he immediately went to France, promising to himself never to return to Ireland or Britain. In France, he wrote his last work, The Ballad of Reading Gaol (1898), a long poem commemorating his harsh prison life. At the age of 46, Wilde died in Paris.

Sigmund Freud

Sigmund Freud (6 May 1856 – 23 September 1939) was an Austrian neurologist, who is the founder of psychoanalysis – a clinical method for treating psychological disorders through dialogue between a patient and a psychoanalyst. Regarded as his greatest contribution, psychoanalysis remains influential within psychology, psychiatry, psychotherapy, and across the humanities. Freud also became popular for his interpretations of people's dreams. However, in order to escape the Nazis, he fled to Austria in 1938. A year later, Freud died in exile in the United Kingdom.

Thomas Woodrow Wilson

Thomas Woodrow Wilson (28 December 1856 – 3 February 1924) was the President of the United States of America during World War I. He was a devoted member of the Presbyterian Church – a branch of Protestant based on the doctrines of John Calvin and governed by elders. What made Wilson famous is his 'Fourteen Points', a statement of principles used for peace negotiations in order to end World War I. In addition, he is known for signing the "Jones Act" on 2 March 1917 which granted United States citizenship to Puerto Ricans. Former President Wilson also showed support for creating Czechoslovakia – a state located in Central Europe which existed from October 1918, until its dissolution into the Czech Republic and Slovakia on January 1993.

Henry Ford

Henry Ford (30 July 1863 – 7 April 1947) was an American industrialist, who founded the Ford Motor Company. He is known as the one who developed and manufactured the first automobile that many middle class Americans could afford. With the success of his company, Ford became one of the richest and best-known people in the world. In addition, he is credited with "Fordism" – mass producing inexpensive goods coupled with high wages for workers. Henry Ford died due to a cerebral hemorrhage on April 7, 1947, at the age of 83. He then left most of his vast wealth to the Ford Foundation and arranged for his family to control the company permanently.

Marie Curie

Marie Curie (7 November 1867 – 4 July 1934) was a Polish physicist and chemist who started the research on radioactivity – the emission of radiation or particles. She is the first woman who has won a Nobel Prize and the first person and only woman to win the said prize twice. In addition, she served as the first woman to become a professor at the University of Paris. Her greatest achievements include: the development of the theory of radioactivity and the discovery of polonium (a rare and highly radioactive metal) and radium (a chemical element). Unfortunately, Curie died in 1934 at the age of 66, due to aplastic anemia – the result of her exposure to radiation while carrying test tubes of radium in her pockets during research, and in mobile X-ray units that she had set up during the World War I to help soldiers.

The Wright Brothers

The Wright brothers Wilbur (16 April 1867 – 30 May 1912) and Orville (19 August 1871 – 30 January 1948) were the ones who developed the first powered aircraft. These brothers were both inventors who are credited for inventing, building and flying the world's first successful airplane. It was in 1904–05 when the brothers developed their airplane.

Mahatma Gandhi

Mohandas Karamchand Gandhi, who is also known as Mahatma Gandhi (2 October 1869 – 30 January 1948) was an Indian nationalist and politician. He believed in non-violent resistance to British rule and helps reconcile Hindu and Muslims. He became famous for leading India to independence and inspiring movements for civil rights and freedom across the world. Because of his contributions to his country, he is unofficially called the Father of the Nation. Gandhi was imprisoned for many years in both South Africa and India. On 30 January 1948, Nathuram Godse, a Hindu nationalist, assassinated Gandhi. Gandhi's birthday, which is the 2nd of October, is commemorated as Gandhi Jayanti – a national holiday in India, which is also known world-wide as the International Day of Nonviolence.

Winston Churchill

Sir Winston Leonard Spencer-Churchill or simply, Winston Churchill (30 November 1874 – 24 January 1965) was the Prime Minister of Great Britain during World War II. Aside from having served as a Prime Minister, he was also an officer in the British Army, a non-academic historian, a writer and an artist. In fact, Churchill won a Nobel Prize in Literature. In addition, he is also the first person to be made an honorary citizen of the United States or a person of exceptional merit. Generally, Churchill gained fame as a war correspondent or journalist and was regarded as one of the most influential people in British history. His greatest contribution was his being an inspiration for British people during World War II. He toured the country inspecting the bomb-damaged towns and cities, tirelessly working to uplift his people to stand up again.

Konrad Adenauer

Konrad Hermann Joseph Adenauer or simply, Konrad Adenauer (5 January 1876 – 19 April 1967) was the first post-war and oldest Chancellor (senior state or legal official) of Germany (West Germany) from 1949 to 1963, at the age of 87. He led his country from the ruins of World War II to a productive nation, as well as in achieving democracy, stability, international respect and economic prosperity. In addition, Adenauer helps his country develop close relationships with France, Great Britain and the United States. He also became the first leader of the Christian Democratic Union (CDU) – the most influential party in Germany.

Albert Einstein

Albert Einstein (1879 – 1955) was a physicist who made ground breaking discoveries in the field of physics. In addition, he was also a humanitarian and peace activist. Although born in Germany, he lived and became a citizen of the US. Generally, Einstein is remembered as the one who developed the general theory of relativity – a theory about gravity. Einstein is also best known for his mass–energy equivalence formula $E = mc2$, which is noted as "the world's most famous equation".

Franklin D. Roosevelt

Franklin Delano Roosevelt who is also known as FDR (30 January 1882 – 12 April 1945) was the US President from 1932 until 1945, who is noted for winning four presidential elections. He was the one who led the US through the Great Depression (a severe worldwide economic depression) and World War II. To help his countrymen, he developed a program for relief, recovery and reform, known as the New Deal –the unemployment rate in the country dropped to 2% and the economy grew rapidly. However, Roosevelt's health deteriorate during the war years, that he died three months into his fourth term. He is also regarded as one of the top three U.S. Presidents.

Coco Chanel

Gabrielle Bonheur "Coco" Chanel or simply, Coco Chanel (19 August 1883 – 10 January 1971) was a French fashion designer and businesswoman, who founded the Chanel brand. Along with Paul Poiret, Chanel was credited in the post-World War I era for popularizing a sporty, casual chic look as the feminine standard of style. Generally, she is considered as the greatest fashion designer who ever lived. Aside from couture clothing, she also designed jewelries, handbags and fragrances, with her signature scent, Chanel No. 5, becoming an iconic product. In 1970, her net worth was US$19 billion, which has a 2015 equivalence of US$118 billion. And so, Coco Chanel was regarded as one of the richest women of all time.

Jawaharlal Nehru

Jawaharlal Nehru (14 November 1889 – 27 May 1964) was the first Indian Prime Minister, who reigned from 1947 until his death in 1964. He led the country towards independence under the guidance and supervision of Mahatma Gandhi. In addition, he is also known in India as Pandit Nehru, while many Indian children knew him as "Uncle Nehru". Nehru was elected by the Congress as India's first Prime Minister, when Gandhi acknowledged him as his political successor. And despite his political difficulties, he remained popular with the people of India. In fact, in his country, his birthday is celebrated as Children's Day.

Dwight D. Eisenhower

Dwight David "Ike" Eisenhower (14 October 1890 – 28 March 1969) was a General of the Army who served as the 34th President of the United States of America (1953-1961). Aside from being a five-star general in the United States Army during World War II, he also served as Supreme Commander of the Allied Forces in Europe. He was the one responsible for the invasion of North Africa, France and Germany. In 1951, he also became the first Supreme Commander of NATO (North Atlantic Treaty Organization) – a military alliance with headquarters based in Belgium. Moreover, it is also Eisenhower who authorized the establishment of NASA (National Aeronautics and Space Administration) – a branch of the US government responsible for space program, aeronautics research and aerospace research. Due to his amazing contributions, he is considered as one of the greatest U.S. Presidents.

Mao Zedong

Mao Zedong or Mao Tse-tung (26 December 1893 – 9 September 1976) was a Chinese revolutionary that became the founding father of the People's Republic of China. He ruled China from 1949 to 1976. He is famous for developing Maoism, a political theory that gives importance to peasantry, small-scale industry and agriculture. His supporters regarded him as the one responsible for modernizing China as well as for making the country a world power that promotes higher status for women and improved education and health care.

Amelia Earhart

Amelia Mary Earhart (24 July 1897 – disappeared 2 July 1937) was an American who was the first female pilot to fly alone across the Atlantic Ocean. For this record, she received the U.S. Distinguished Flying Cross – a military decoration awarded to those who made extraordinary achievement while participating in an aerial flight. Aside from being a pilot, Earhart is also an author who wrote best-selling books about her flying experiences. Unfortunately, in 1937, during her attempt to make a circumnavigational flight of the globe, Earhart disappeared over the Pacific Ocean. Up to this day, her disappearance remains a mystery.

Walt Disney

Walter Elias "Walt" Disney or simply, Walt Disney (5 December 1901 – 15 December 1966) was an American entrepreneur, animator, voice actor and film producer. He was the one who started the American animation industry. Overall, he had 22 Academy Awards and has won more Oscars awards than anyone else. It was in 1920s when he set up the Disney Brothers Studio (later The Walt Disney Company) with his brother Roy. He developed the Mickey Mouse character in 1928. Mickey Mouse served as Disney's first highly popular character. Some of his famous films include: *Snow White and the Seven Dwarfs, Pinocchio, Dumbo* and *Cinderella.* In 1955, Disney opened the first Disneyland.

Mother Teresa

Mother Teresa or Saint Teresa of Calcutta (26 August 1910 – 5 September 1997) was an Albanian-born Catholic nun. She went to India where she lived for most of her life to serve the poor. In addition, she also organized: hospices; homes for people with HIV/AIDS, leprosy and tuberculosis; soup kitchens; mobile clinics; counseling programs; orphanages; and schools. These charitable works of her are what made Mother Teresa a symbol of charity and humanitarian sacrifice. She received a Nobel Peace Prize in 1979. Mother Theresa was recognized as "Blessed Teresa of Calcutta" in 19 October 2003 and was canonized as a saint by the Roman Catholic Church on 4 September 2016.

Ronald Reagan

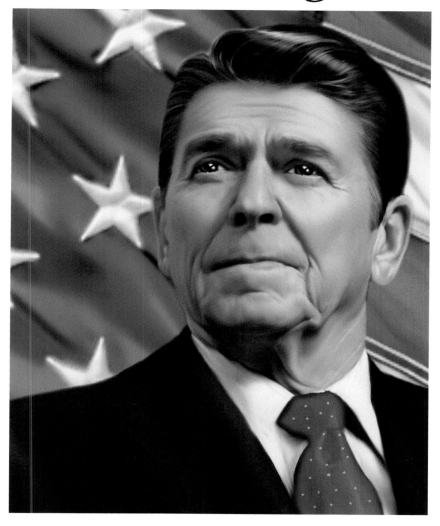

Ronald Wilson Reagan (6 February 1911 – 5 June 2004) was an American politician and actor who served as the US President from 1981 until 1989. He was noted for the speech, "A Time for Choosing" he delivered in 1964 to support Barry Goldwater's presidential campaign. Not long after, in 1966, Reagan was elected Governor of California, and was re-elected in 1970. It was in 1981 when he won presidency. His contributions to his country include: tax rate reduction, economic deregulation and reduction in government spending. As he finished his term as the US President, Reagan got an approval rating of 68%.

John F. Kennedy

John Fitzgerald "Jack" Kennedy or JFK (29 May 1917 – 22 November 1963) was the US President from 1961 until 1963. At age of 43, he was regarded as the second-youngest president. Kennedy is the only Roman Catholic president. During his inauguration as the 35th US President, he spoke the famous saying: "Ask not what your country can do for you; ask what you can do for your country". During his term, Kennedy ordered the Bay of Pigs Invasion – a failed military invasion of Cuba by the US in order to overthrow the communist government of Fidel Castro. In addition, he was also the one who created the Peace Corps – a volunteer program by the US government to help people outside the country to understand American culture, and to also help Americans understand the cultures of other countries. On 22 November 1963, Kennedy was assassinated in Dallas, Texas.

Nelson Mandela

Nelson Rolihlahla Mandela or simply, Nelson Mandela (18 July 1918 – 5 December 2013) was the first President of South Africa (1994-1999). He became famous for his involvement in the 1952 anti-apartheid Defiance Campaign – a campaign to protest the apartheid laws or the racial segregation in South Africa that favors the white inhabitants of the country. In addition, Mandela also established a militant group that fought the government. Because of this, Mandela was arrested in 1962 for conspiring to overthrow the state. He was sentenced to life imprisonment but only served 27 years in prison after his release on 1990. Nelson Mandela received several awards, including: Nobel Peace Prize, U.S. Presidential Medal of Freedom, and Soviet Lenin Peace Prize, for his work for the peaceful termination of the apartheid regime. In South Africa, he is honored with deep respect, is called Tata ("Father"), and described as the "Father of the Nation".

Pope John Paul II

Pope Saint John Paul II or Saint John Paul the Great (18 May 1920 – 2 April 2005) was a Polish Pope from 1978 to 2005. He is known for bringing together different religions by improving Catholic Church's relations with Judaism, Islam, the Eastern Orthodox Church, and the Anglican Communion. He also played a significant role in the end of communism in Eastern Europe. Communism is a system in which mines, factories, and farms in the society are owned by the public or the state, and wealth is divided among citizens equally or according to individual need. Moreover, Pope John Paul II is also considered one of the most travelled world leaders in history – visiting 129 countries during his term as a Pope. Due to his contributions, John Paul II was officially declared as a saint by the Roman Catholic Church on 27 April 2014.

Margaret Thatcher

Margaret Hilda Thatcher (13 October 1925 – 8 April 2013) was a British politician and who became the United Kingdom's Prime Minister from 4 May 1979 – 28 November 1990. She was considered as the longest-serving British prime minister of the 20th century. She was also regarded as the first woman to become the country's Prime Minister. During her term as the Prime Minister, she implemented Thatcherism – a series of political and economic initiatives to decrease unemployment rates and increase Britain's economy by privatization of state-owned industries, centralizing power from local authorities to central government and controlling the supply of money.

Queen Elizabeth II

Queen Elizabeth II who was born in 21 April 1926 is the queen of the United Kingdom from 6 February 1952 up to present. She also served as the Queen of Canada, Australia, and New Zealand, and as the Head of the Commonwealth. In addition, Queen Elizabeth is, as well, Queen of 12 other countries including: Jamaica, Barbados, the Bahamas, Grenada, Papua New Guinea, Solomon Islands, Tuvalu, Saint Lucia, Saint Vincent and the Grenadines, Belize, Antigua and Barbuda, and Saint Kitts and Nevis. These countries are members of the Commonwealth of Nations (organization of states that are parts of the former British Empire), which have Queen Elizabeth II as the reigning constitutional monarch. In 1947, she married Philip, Duke of Edinburgh, and had four children: Charles, Anne, Andrew, and Edward. At the age of 90, she is regarded as the world's oldest reigning monarch as well as the longest-reigning British monarch. Amazingly, the support for her monarchy remains high, as does her personal popularity.

Marilyn Monroe

Marilyn Monroe (1 June 1926 – 5 August 1962) was an American actress and model, who become popular for playing "dumb blonde" characters. By 1953, she became one of the most bankable Hollywood stars. He played leading roles in three films: the noir Niagara, Gentlemen Prefer Blondes and How to Marry a Millionaire. In 1959, she won a Golden Globe for Best Actress for the film, *Some Like It Hot*. Although her career lasted for only a decade, Monroe's films grossed $200 million by the time of her unexpected death in 1962.

Martin Luther King Jr.

Martin Luther King (15 January 1929 – 4 April 1968) was an American Baptist minister and activist. He was the leader of the American Civil Rights Movement, a non-violent civil rights movement. He helped in organizing the 1963 March on Washington – one of the largest rallies for human rights that demanded civil and economic rights for African Americans. This is where King delivered his famous "I Have a Dream" speech in which he called for an end to racism. There, he also established his reputation as one of the greatest orators in American history. Because of his non-violent protest against racial inequality, he was given a Nobel Peace Prize on October 14, 1964. When he was assassinated on 4 April1968 in Memphis, Tennessee, many riots happened in most U.S. cities.

Audrey Hepburn

Audrey Kathleen Ruston, who is more commonly known as Audrey Hepburn (4 May 1929 – 20 January 1993) was a British actress regarded as a film and fashion icon. She was ranked as the third-greatest female screen legend. Her popularity started when she played the lead role in Roman Holiday (1953), where she won an Academy Award, a Golden Globe Award and a BAFTA Award for a single performance. Since then, she went on to star in several successful films including: *Sabrina (1954), The Nun's Story (1959), Breakfast at Tiffany's (1961), Charade (1963), My Fair Lady (1964) and Wait Until Dark (1967)*. However, as Hepburn ages, she devoted much of her time to UNICEF and in helping the poorest communities of Africa, South America and Asia. In 1992, she was given the Presidential Medal of Freedom.

Anne Frank

Annelies Marie Frank or simply, Anne Frank (12 June 1929 – February or March 1945) was a German-born diarist and writer. She is one of the most popular Jewish victims of the Holocaust, in which Adolf Hitler's Nazi Germany killed about six million Jews. Her famous diary, *The Diary of a Young Girl*, documents her life as she hides during the German occupation in World War II. Her diary is one of the world's most widely known books. From Germany, her family moved to the Netherlands where they hide in some concealed rooms behind a bookcase in the building where Anne's father worked. However, in August 1944, they were betrayed and transported to German's camps. Anne and her sister, Margot, were eventually transferred to a different camp, where they died in February or March 1945.

Mikhail Gorbachev

Mikhail Sergeyevich Gorbachev who was born on 2 March 1931 was the eighth and last leader of the Soviet Union or USSR, a socialist state on the Eurasian continent that existed from 1922 to 1991. His policies of glasnost or "openness" and perestroika or "restructuring" contributed to the end of the Cold War – a tension after World War II between the United States (and its allies) and the Soviet Union (and its allies). He was also the one responsible for the dissolution of the Soviet Union. He was awarded the Otto Hahn Peace Medal in 1989, the Nobel Peace Prize in 1990 and the Harvey Prize in 1992.

Elvis Presley

Elvis Aaron Presley or simply, Elvis Presley (8 January 1935 – 16 August 1977) was an American musician and actor. He was regarded as the leading figure of rock and roll and one of the most significant icons of the 20th century. He is also often regarded as the "King of Rock and Roll". His energized interpretations of songs and provocative performance style, made him very popular. Overall, Presley is considered as the best-selling solo artist in the history of recorded music. He has estimated record sales of around 600 million units worldwide and has won several Grammy Awards. As an actor, he made his first film in November 1956, which is entitled, Love Me Tender. Unfortunately, in 1977, Elvis Presley died at the age of 42 due to severely damaged health as a result of several years of prescription drug abuse.

14th Dalai Lama

The 14th Dalai Lama or Tenzin Gyatso, who was born on 6 July 1935, is the current Dalai Lama or monk of the Tibetan Buddhism. He also served as the spiritual and political leader of Tibetans. He is a leading figure for non-violence and spirituality. He traveled all over the world to speak about the welfare of Tibetans, non-violence, women's rights, physics, astronomy, Buddhism and science, reproductive health, and sexuality. During the 1959 Tibetan Uprising or 1959 Tibetan Rebellion, when the Chinese army invades Tibet, the Dalai Lama fled to India, where he currently lives as a refugee. Due to his non-violent advocacy, the 14th Dalai Lama received the Nobel Peace Prize in 1989.

Pope Francis

Jorge Mario Bergoglio or Pope Francis (born on 17 December 1936) is the current Pope of the Roman Catholic Church. He is the first Jesuit pope and the first one who came from the Americas. Before he entered seminary studies, he used to work as a chemical technologist and a nightclub bouncer. When Pope Benedict XVI resigned as a pope on 28 February 2013, Bergoglio was elected as his successor on 13 March 2013. The focus of his papacy supports taking action on climate change. He is also known to have a humble and less formal approach to the papacy than his predecessors, explaining that the church should be more open and welcoming.

John Lennon

John Winston Ono Lennon or simply, John Lennon (9 October 1940 – 8 December 1980) was an English singer and songwriter. He co-founded the Beatles (a popular English rock band), which is considered as the most commercially successful band in the history of popular music. When the band was dissolved in 1970, Lennon went on a solo career and produced the songs such as "Give Peace a Chance", "Working Class Hero", and "Imagine". In 1975, Lennon left the music industry for a while to raise his infant son Sean. He re-entered the music world in 1980 with the new album Double Fantasy. Three weeks after the release of his new album, Lennon was murdered. But despite his death, Lennon's solo album sales in the United States exceeded 14 million as of 2012.

Muhammad Ali

Muhammad Ali (7 January 1942 – 3 June 2016) is a famous American boxer and a leading figure in the civil rights movement. From Cassius Clay, which he called his "slave name", he changed his legal name to Muhammad Ali, which symbolized his resistance to white domination during the 1960s Civil Rights Movement. His objection to support the United States of America in the Vietnam War is what made him an icon. After retiring from boxing in 1981, Muhammad Ali devoted his life to religious and charitable work. However, in 1984, he was diagnosed with Parkinson's syndrome, which eventually led to his death on June 3, 2016 in Scottsdale, Arizona.

Billie Jean King

Billie Jean King is an American who was born on 22 November 1943, was once considered as the world's no. 1 professional tennis player. She won 39 Grand Slam titles and was the United States' captain in the Federation Cup (international team competition in women's tennis) for three years. Aside from being an excellent tennis player, King is also an advocate for gender equality and was the founder of the Women's Tennis Association and the Women's Sports Foundation. King received numerous awards due to her contributions in the sport's and tennis' world. Some of her awards include: International Tennis Hall of Fame in 1987 and National Women's Hall of Fame in 1990 and in 2006.

Aung San Suu Kyi

Aung San Suu Kyi, who was born on 19 June 1945, is a Burmese politician, diplomat and author who was the First and current Leader of the National League for Democracy – a political party in Myanmar. In addition, she is also known as the first female Minister of Foreign Affairs of Myanmar and the Minister of President's Office. Although she was prohibited from becoming the President, as her late husband and children are foreign citizens, she became Burma's State Councilor, a role similar to a Prime Minister. For her non-violent struggle for democracy and human rights, Aung San Suu Kyi also received many honors, including: Nobel Peace Prize, Rafto Prize, Jawaharlal Nehru Award, Sakharov Prize, US Congressional Gold Medal, and Presidential Medal of Freedom.

Prince Charles

Charles, Prince of Wales or Prince Charles (born on 14 November 1948) is the eldest child of Queen Elizabeth II. He also bore the titles: Duke of Rothesay and Duke of Cornwall. He is considered as the oldest person to be next in line to the throne since Sophia of Hanover, the heir of Queen Anne. He married Lady Diana Spencer in 1981and had two sons: Prince William and Prince Harry. However, the royal couple divorced in 1996. In 2005, Prince Charles re-married, this time to Camilla Parker Bowles. Prince Charles was renowned for his charitable works. He founded The Prince's Trust in 1976, sponsors The Prince's Charities and is patron of numerous other charitable and arts organizations. In addition, he is also an environmentalist that promotes organic farming for which he established the Duchy Home Farm. Aside from farming, he also raises world awareness on the dangers brought by climate change.

Oprah Winfrey

Oprah Gail Winfrey who was born on 29 January 1954, is an American media proprietor, producer, talk show host and actress. Her talk show "The Oprah Winfrey Show", which was the highest-rated television program of its kind in history, is what made her very popular. She is also regarded as the "Queen of All Media" and was ranked the richest African-American of the 20th century. Currently, she is the first and only multi-billionaire African American in North America. On January 2011, Oprah Winfrey founded the Oprah Winfrey Network, an American television channel.

Steve Jobs

Steven Paul Jobs, who is more commonly known as Steve Jobs (24 February 1955 – 5 October 2011) was an American entrepreneur and inventor. He was the co-founder of Apple Inc., a majority shareholder of Pixar Animation Studios; a member of The Walt Disney Company's board of directors and founder of NeXT Inc. In 1976, he co-founded Apple with Steve Wozniak to sell personal computers. A year later, they became famous and wealthy. However, due to a power struggle within the company, Jobs was forced out of Apple in 1985. After leaving Apple, Jobs took a few of its members with him to found NeXT – a company which specializes in state-of-the-art computers for higher-education and business markets. In 1997, Apple purchased NeXT and Jobs became the CEO of the company. He saved Apple from bankruptcy and develops a new line of products including: iMac, iTunes, Apple Stores, the iPod, the iTunes Store, the iPhone, the App Store, and the iPad. Unfortunately, Jobs was diagnosed with a pancreatic neuroendocrine tumor in 2003, which led to his death on 2011.

Bill Gates

William Henry "Bill" Gates III or simply, Bill Gates (born on 28 October 1955) is an American businessman, philanthropist, investor and programmer. Together with Paul Allen, he co-founded Microsoft in 1975. Eventually, Microsoft became the world's largest PC software company. He also authored and co-authored several books. Due to his undeniable success, Gates is included in the Forbes list of the world's wealthiest people since 1987. He is considered as the wealthiest person in the world from 1995 to 2007, in 2009 and from 2014 onwards. As of August 2016, he has a net worth of US$78.3 billion. However, large amounts of his money were given to several charitable organizations and scientific research programs through the Bill & Melinda Gates Foundation.

Madonna

Madonna Louise Ciccone or simply, Madonna (born on 16 August 1958) is an American actress, dancer, singer, songwriter and businesswoman. She is well known for reinventing both her music and image, and for maintaining her autonomy within the recording industry. She is also referred to as the "Queen of Pop". Throughout her career, she has written and produced most of her songs. Many of her songs topped the record charts, including: "Like a Virgin", "Papa Don't Preach", "Like a Prayer", "Vogue", "Take a Bow", "Frozen", "Music", "Hung Up", and "4 Minutes". With more than 300 million records worldwide, Madonna became the best-selling female recording artist of all time by Guinness World Records. Her other ventures include acting, fashion designing, writing children's books, and filmmaking.

Michael Jackson

Michael Joseph Jackson or Michael Jackson (29 August 1958 – 25 June 2009) was an American dancer, record producer, singer, songwriter and actor. He is called the "King of Pop". His album Thriller is the best-selling album of all time, with estimated sales of 65 million copies worldwide. He is also recognized as the Most Successful Entertainer of All Time by Guinness World Records. Throughout his career, Jackson received so many awards including: multiple Guinness World Records, 13 Grammy Awards and 26 American Music Awards. In 2002, the Guinness World Records recognized him for supporting 39 charities, more than any other entertainer. Unfortunately, while preparing for his comeback concerts, Michael Jackson died of substance intoxication on 25 June 2009, after suffering from cardiac arrest. Forbes ranks Jackson as the top-earning dead celebrity, with US$115 million in earnings.

Princess Diana

Princess Diana (1 July 1961 – 31 August 1997) was the first wife of Prince Charles, the eldest child of Queen Elizabeth II. While married, Diana bore the titles Princess of Wales, Duchess of Cornwall, Duchess of Rothesay, Countess of Chester, and Baroness of Renfrew. She has two sons: Prince William and Prince Harry. She was well known for her charity works and support of the International Campaign to Ban Landmines. However, on 31 August 1997, Princess Diana died in a car crash in Paris, resulting in extensive mourning by the public.

Michael Jordan

Michael Jeffrey Jordan or Michael Jordan, who was born on 17 February 1963, is an American retired professional basketball player and a businessman, who is the principal owner and chairman of the Charlotte Hornets. In 2015, as an owner of an NBA franchise, he became the first billionaire NBA player in history and the world's second-richest African-American. In addition, Jordan is regarded as the greatest basketball player of all time and was considered to play a significant role in popularizing the NBA around the world during the 1980s and 1990s. He was also best known for his prolific scoring and leaping ability, which earned him the nicknames "Air Jordan" and "His Airness".

J.K Rowling

Joanne Rowling, or J. K. Rowling (born on 31 July 1965) is a British novelist, screenwriter and film producer. She was renowned and very well known as the author of the Harry Potter fantasy series. These particular books became popular and even won multiple awards. In total, more than 400 million copies of Harry Potter books were sold, making it the best-selling book series in history. After the last sequel of the Harry Potter series, in 2007, Rowling has since written four books for adult readers under the pseudonym Robert Galbraith. Living a true-to-life story of "rags to riches", Rowling progressed from being very poor to multi-millionaire status within five years. Currently, she is considered as the United Kingdom's best-selling living author.

David Beckham

David Robert Joseph Beckham or simply, David Beckham (born on 2 May 1975) is a former professional football player. He played for several football teams including: Manchester United, Real Madrid, Preston North End, Paris Saint-Germain, Milan, LA Galaxy, and the England national team. He is also notable for being the first English player to win league titles in four countries: England, Spain, US and France. However, Beckham retired in 2013 after 20 years of playing football. Overall, he won 19 major trophies and was listed as one of the highest-paid players in the world. He is married to Victoria Beckham and has four children. Since 2009, the football star serves a UNICEF UK ambassador. The UNICEF or the United Nations Children's Emergency Fund is a United Nations program that provides long-term humanitarian and developmental assistance to children and mothers.

Michael Phelps

Michael Fred Phelps II or simply, Michael Phelps (born on 30 June 1985) is an American swimmer considered as the most decorated Olympian of all time, with a total of 28 medals. He holds the all-time records for Olympic gold medals (28). Unbelievably, he won eight gold medals at the 2008 Beijing Games, 4 gold medals at the 2012 London Olympics and five gold medals at the 2016 Rio Olympics. In total, Phelps has 66 gold medals, 14 silver medals and 3 bronze medals which he won at the Olympics, the World, and the Pan Pacific Championships. With his international titles and record-breaking, he was given the World Swimmer of the Year Award seven times and American Swimmer of the Year Award nine times as well as the FINA Swimmer of the Year Award in 2012.

Usain Bolt

Usain St. Leo Bolt or simply, Usain Bolt (born on 21 August 1986) is a Jamaican sprinter. He is regarded as the fastest human ever timed. He is also the first one to hold both the 100 meters and 200 meters world records. Amazingly, he too holds the world record in the 4 × 100 meters relay. Currently, he is the reigning World and Olympic champion in the said three events. Unbelievably, Bolt is a nine-time Olympic gold medalist and an eleven-time World Champion. With his achievements in sprinting, he was nicknamed "Lightning Bolt". However, the great athlete stated that he intends to retire from athletics after the 2017 World Championships.

CPSIA information can be obtained at www.ICGtesting.com
Printed in the USA
LVIW01n1532291116
514955LV00015B/110